# LEADERSHIP

BEST PRACTICES AND PROCESSES
FOR IN-HOUSE CREATIVE LEADERS

Acknowledgements

This book is dedicated to all the fearless in-house creative leaders out there. Thank you to all who made this book a fun and seamless process.


Content Contributors

| | |
|---|---|
| Editorial Director | Kim Kiser |
| Copy Editor | Vivian Fransen |
| 2-Minute Tips | Chris Davies |
| | Robin Colangelo |
| Articles | Andy Brenits |
| | Bob Calvano |
| | Nathalie Heywood |
| | Glenn Gontha |
| | Ed Roberts |
| | Brandie Knox |
| | Cynthia Saccoman |
| | Chris Davies |
| | Joe Staples |
| | Angela Buchanico |
| Interview | Kevin Kearns |

"Leadership" is the first edition of something greater to come.
A pre-published brain dump to inspire you before the big reveal.

ISBN-13: 978-1530254927
ISBN-10: 1530254922

**in-source.org**

**Welcome.** Inside you'll find fresh ideas to spark your inspiration in creative leadership, brand management and strategic design to help you solve today's business challenges.

This compilation of thought leadership articles, tips and an exclusive interview was created by a group of in-house design leaders who believe in supporting and evolving the efforts of in-house design.

For more than 10 years, InSource has been committed to creative leadership excellence and effective business management, with a focus on providing a platform to share ideas and practices among leaders of in-house creative teams. Our goal is to enhance the value in-house creative teams add to their organizations and brands.

InSource has expanded its reach to thousands of creative professionals around the world through our online channels and events. We are able to offer our members relevant information on topics relating to real-life, in-house creative leadership challenges.

Visit our website at in-source.org for more information on how you can consider InSource a valuable resource for you and your in-house creative team.

We hope you'll enjoy this collection of practical insights as one of the many ways we reach out to each another as peers in our ongoing pursuit of design management excellence.

**Andy Brenits**
President, InSource

**Robin Colangelo**
Vice President, InSource

# The In-House Business
## Start-Up Journal

-Andy Brenits

Based on my experiences in managing creative services start-up operations for four organizations in my 20+ year career, this article is an amalgamation of my lessons learned from leading creative services businesses and from the trials and tribulations of getting things up and running to a sustainable state. Names have been changed to protect the innocent or those who should have known better.

### The new guy in town

I've had the privilege of starting a new job 11 times in my career, which includes some part-time, after-hours teaching gigs. So I've seen a wide gamut of orientation and on-boarding programs. Some have been great, others have been less than great.

I've also seen the lack of any orientation and on-boarding, and I think it's quite telling about an organization when your first few days on the job don't have any formal structure around getting you up to speed on who's who and what's what.

In running a business of any kind, it's important to remember that you, as a manager, have only three resources at your disposal—money, people and information. When someone starts a new job, he or she needs one of those three things more than the others: information. Who are the people who report to you? Who are your stakeholders? What's your budget? What are the company policies? How do I get in touch with IT tech support? What are the tools you need to use? What's the process for engaging the team? What work takes priority? You need answers to all these questions.

As a start-up organization, however, none of these things may exist yet. So it's going to be your job to figure it all out on behalf of other people.

Just don't do anything in an ad hoc way. Keep organized and be methodical in assessing the situation, so that you can put all the pieces together and get the ship on course.

### Talking less and listening more

My first few days on the job typically involve meeting lots of new people, including colleagues, clients, executives and direct reports. Along with the usual and customary "welcome aboard" handshaking, I'm also asked about my background and experience.

Over the next few days as I meet more people and begin to feel comfortable with the ones I've already met, I also start learning more about how things are currently operating, or how things used to be. I probably don't have to tell you that people in any office setting love to talk about the good old days, especially when they were not all that good.

Anyone who knows me knows that I'm a talker. However, an important part of managing and leading is active listening. And that's what I'm doing more of during my first 10 to 20 days on the job than at any other time. It's not just the formal meetings with my boss, his/her boss, clients and stakeholders, as well as department colleagues, that give me the knowledge I'm going to need, but all of the impromptu gatherings, office drop-bys, first-week-on-the-job lunches and hallway meetings that really inform me about what I need to do.

I learn more about what is or isn't working, or needs to be implemented, from these short conversations than almost any other time on the job. And I use these opportunities to ask questions and really listen to the answers my co-workers give me about how my team can be most effective.

### Assessment and planning at less than warp speed

The first task I undertake when starting a new creative services leadership job is to assess the situation. After about a month, I typically have a good understanding of what's going on so I can start putting together my big plan for the department. While I want to be careful not to overgeneralize, I can still pretty much categorize any current state of affairs into one of three scenarios:

**one:**   The current creative services process and infrastructure are working, but need to be fine-tuned to best serve our clients.

**two:**   The current creative services process and infrastructure are not working and need a top-to-bottom retooling.

**three:**   There are no discernable creative services process and infrastructure, and they need to be established.

Each of these scenarios provides its own unique challenges, and any plan I put together will absolutely require buy-in from my boss, my team and our clients in order to be successful. But if there is one thing I've learned over the years, it's that you can't change too much, too fast. Sure, people say they want change, and leaders have even recognized change is needed. But things have been working a certain way—good, bad or otherwise—since before I came onto the scene. So change can end up being disruptive, destructive and counterproductive, if handled in a cavalier manner.

While my gut tells me we need to flip a switch on Monday and have things work in a new way, my experience—and observations of human behavior—tells me that change really needs to be incremental. Otherwise, I'm at risk for clients getting things done the way they used to, undermining the new process and potentially compromising the company's strategic plans.

Sometimes when developing a change implementation plan, dialing it down from 11 to 6 is a good thing.

### Planning the rollout

After a couple months of planning, the time has come to institute the plans that I have been developing since the day I started. I've built some key relationships, assessed a few situations, identified needs, designed processes and (I hope) built some trust. Now all I need to do is stop talking about the "big plan" and start getting it going already.

Having done this a few times, I know there are a few ways to roll out new processes and SOPs. I have learned from experience there is a definite wrong way to do it—that is, to flip the switch. As soon as you introduce even the smallest change factor in how people work, you throw them into a period of turbulence that will take time to normalize. Check out Bruce Tuckman's Group Development Model ("Developmental sequence in small groups," Psychological Bulletin, 63, 384-399) of forming, storming, norming, and performing.

Change can be a tough thing to manage, and it's really a matter of giving people time to absorb changes slowly. In the case of an in-house business, three groups of people need to learn and embrace your changes: your boss(es), your clients and your staff.

Change is good, or so I've been told. But too much change, too fast, can be disastrous. So what's an impulsive, go-with-my-gut-kind-of-guy to do? Slow down and take a phased approach. Embrace the idea of soft-launching the new processes to test them out, and then make revisions before the big rollout.

### No one will come to your party, unless you invite them

Like any business that is launching new products or services, all of the planning and development we have put into the new creative services department will have been for naught, if we don't announce the launch of new processes to our clients. Here's an email from our department to others in corporate communications who request our services:

Good morning, everyone,

Since March we have been analyzing Creative Services' existing processes, capabilities and needs along with those of our clients—both within and outside of the department.

There have been a number of behind-the-scenes improvements on how we collectively work to produce creative deliverables. While we hope that some of these behind-the-scenes changes are already noticeable to everyone, today we have an exciting announcement that we think everyone will appreciate.

Beginning today there is a new centralized point of contact for all creative services requests (e.g., graphic design, photography, video production and brand identity review). Simply send an email to our department by typing "Creative Services" in the "To..." field of your email, and it will go to our department's general mailbox.

From there someone will review your request, ask for more information as needed and assign a creative professional to assist you. You will receive an email with our project reference number, and who your assigned creative services contact will be. When initiating a new creative project of any kind, please feel free to use the attached Creative Services Request Sheet. Additionally, if you are requesting video production assistance, you may find the attached Video Production Project Sheet useful in planning your production timing and script.

While neither tool is mandatory to use, they will allow us to more effectively, and efficiently, get the project opened and into our production queue. Plus, you may just find them helpful in collecting, and communicating to us, the details of your project prior to requesting creative consultation and assistance.

If you have any questions or comments, please do not hesitate to call me, or drop by my office.

Andy Brenits
Leader, Creative Services

What's important about this message is not so much all of the behind-the-scenes process development we have undertaken that will make the new creative services team more effective and creative, but the fact that it addresses only the two most common pain points clients complained about when I began my analysis and planning work:

+ They don't know how to get someone in creative services to help them.

+ They don't know what information to provide when asking for creative consultation.

Providing solutions to these two challenges can be such a big paradigm shift for clients to embrace so we really only call this our soft launch. The big changes are still to come...in the BIG launch a couple of months down the road.

### Sell the work, not the process

Any in-house creative services leader knows that process is important—from how clients initiate new projects to how the team gets work done. It's a very important way to manage workflow, effectiveness, productivity and frankly...order. If we have done our jobs well, things run smoothly for the most part. Clients are happy, designers are engaged and creative, things are good.

Often a creative manager finds that processes need to be improved—or created in the first place—in order to get things running in an optimal state. But developing the new process is only half the battle. You have to sell it to other leaders to get buy-in, and educate colleagues and clients on how things now work. The education of clients can sometimes be painful for those less willing to embrace change, so it can take months of hard work to keep the train from derailing off the tracks you have set. There will come a point in time, however, when the hard sell of the process needs to give way to the soft sell, by proving that the process you put in place works better than how things used to be. You'll be able to prove the new processes work when you can demonstrate the results. I'm talking, of course, about showing off the creative work of your team.

We all desire for our in-house teams to be seen as the go-to resources and creative experts within the company. The best way to do that isn't going to be showing how the work gets done, but rather the work itself. Creative leaders need to find the right opportunities to show how their teams are solving creative problems and contributing to the corporate strategy.

Show off a recent piece of high-quality work in your leadership meeting. Participate in another department's staff meeting and bring samples of completed projects. Build a portfolio website or capabilities brochure and drive traffic to the site. These are a few things you can do to show off the value of your team.

### Admitting mistakes
"Steve Jobs would never have done that," I thought to myself as I read the open apology by Tim Cook regarding the new Maps app in iOS6. As I said those words, I realized that I don't actually think that Tim Cook was wrong to do it though. While not the approach that Jobs would have taken, Cook did something few leaders are bold enough to do—admit when they make a mistake.

As a business leader, I realize the all-important role of earning the respect of my peers, co-workers and clients. However, I think too few leaders also realize the importance of earning the respect of their own teams. There are, of course, many ways to do this such as giving recognition, rewarding and standing up for your team. I also think showing that you're a mere mortal—fallible and someone who occasionally makes bad decisions—is just as important. In my effort to be a transparent leader, I'll share with you an example of how I admitted a recent mistake.

After months of research, demonstrations and RFPs, I decided to purchase a workflow management system (something we desperately needed). All of the demos with the sales representatives made this particular piece of software look like it was the perfect solution. I touted to my boss and my team how this product was the best one based on cost, usability and features. But once it was implemented, it was virtually unusable by my team.

For the first two weeks I repeated, "You're just not used to it yet; give it a chance." For the second two weeks I found myself saying "Let's add that to the list and see if their developer can create a work-around." On the fifth week of complaints, after trying to use the product myself the way they had been (using the simplest of features: time sheets), I called one of the other companies I looked at and fast-tracked the purchase and implementation of their (better) product. The announcement that we would be switching to this other product brought smiles to everyone's faces.

**Here is where I went wrong, and what I admitted to:**
I thought with my budget first. I thought spending $1,600 was better than spending $4,000. You know what, you get what you pay for.

+ I went with a product that seemed easy to use, but wasn't. I should have asked for a free month to play with the system.

+ I didn't listen to my team, even though they are the ones using it most often.

The last point is important, because when I reviewed my notes on my search for the workflow tool, it seems they mentioned they had used the tool we ended up switching to, or at least had heard of it. Likewise, when I polled my industry colleagues, no one seemed to have heard of the product I chose, or they outright told me they disqualified it from their list of choices for a variety of reasons.

So after just a month of use, I offered up a mea culpa to my boss and my team. And you know what? I think I came out looking much better for it as a manager and a leader. Are you brave enough to admit it when you make a mistake?

## Performance reviews

Well, it's that time of year again for many corporate creatives: The year-end performance review cycle has begun again. Unlike many of my colleagues on the outside, I need to follow a prescribed process in which I self-evaluate my performance against several goals (SMART ones) for both the business and my own professional development.

As if providing an evaluation to my boss about my own work wasn't hard enough, I'll also need to review the evaluations my staff wrote about themselves. And if I'm very lucky, no one has any delusions of grandeur about their accomplishments (or lack thereof), including me.

Unfortunately, as a manager, there does come the time when you need to deliver some not-so-good news to an employee about his or her performance. But if you've done your job as a manager, it should not come as a surprise when you do. While formal performance reviews—often coupled with ratings ranging from "needs improvement" to "exceeds expectations"—are conducted twice per year, you should still be having regular conversations with your staff about how they are doing, whether it's to offer praise for a job well done or counseling for an issue of some kind.

You can't be afraid to give those negative reviews. To be blunt, it's how you justify the termination of someone who isn't pulling his or her weight. Or in the case of a headcount reduction, the poor performers are shown the door before a solid one is.

On the upside, a good performance review is just as gratifying to give as it is to receive. If you've been having regular conversations with your staff, catching the small mishaps before they become big performance issues, then you're likely to have mostly positive reviews to give.

### Goal setting

How many of us set New Year's resolutions around December 31st, only to forget them by January 3rd? To avoid treating goal setting like New Year's resolutions, here is something I share with my team every year.

**How to write SMART goals of your own:** Writing SMART goals will ensure a higher degree of success at achieving your goals. SMART goals meet the following criteria:

+ Specific - clear, unambiguous language
+ Measurable - ability to measure progress and achievement
+ Attainable - within the control of the individual or the team
+ Realistic - take into account the individual's present skills and capacity
+ Time-bound - within a defined period of time

As you write your goals make sure that they are SMART and easily defined by what it is, why it is important, how the goal is going to be accomplished and when it will be accomplished by. Having these components clearly identified will assist in the recognition of progress and measurement toward the successful completion of the goal.

For example, a good—but not SMART—goal would be: To lose weight.

A SMART version of this goal looks like this: To lose 20 pounds by November 1st, I will eat healthier and exercise every day in order to fit into my old 36-inch waist jeans. This SMART goal above is constructed using the following sample model for the structure of a SMART goal.

To (the action you will take), by (date/timeframe), I will (do what?) by (a measure you can track) in order to (your real goal).

To lose 20 pounds by November 1st, I will eat healthier and exercise every day in order to fit into my old 36-inch waist jeans.

Good luck!

### Recognition and reward

For many in-house employees, year-end reviews are typically followed by an announcement of merit increases (aka raises) and incentive payouts (aka bonuses). As managers, we often wrestle with the balance of following the corporate guidelines for cash awards with the subjectivity of what constitutes a good job by our creative people.

However, it's important to remember we have more ways to reward employees for good work than yearly raises, bonuses or even promotions.

Recognition comes in many forms, and sometimes a simple "thank-you" for a job well done can pay big dividends in loyalty, motivation and assurance of continued good work. The late Robert Townsend, CEO of AVIS and author of Up the Organization, called the phrase "thank you" a "really neglected form of compensation."

For example, I recently showed off some of the work my team produced in a management team meeting. When I shared the positive responses from my peers with my team, it was clear how much they appreciated not just the accolades, but that I even showed the work off to begin with. This cost me nothing in terms of dollars, but paid off big time with my team.

If you have any budget dollars for training and development, then consider sending someone to a class. If your budget is limited, then send only one high-performing person, but have that person teach what they learned to the rest of your team. This approach yields a three-fold return if you think about it: special recognition for the high performer in terms of the training, a leadership development opportunity for the same person to teach others the new skills and staff development for the others taught by the high performer.

Finally, if you work for a corporation with good perks such as seats at a sports arena, take your team out after work to a big game. Trust me, the joy (and appreciative looks) on their faces will be an immediate reward for you.

### Failure is an option
No, the title is not a mistake. Sometimes you have to let things fail.

I've started and led three creative businesses in my career: two with in-house teams and one agency. I've also been a part of a few business reorganizations in both design practice and academia.

Our in-house business is like any other in that we need to keep trying new things in order to make progress. Sometimes it's a new creative iteration of the brand, sometimes it's a process. Sometimes, if you're fortunate, things work the way you planned. But sometimes they don't. That's a fact of life.

They key is, don't let failure stop you from trying anything. You have to keep trying new things until you have success, and then you move on to find ways to further improve or grow. So whether it's how you manage your team or your clients, or even how you try to instill organizational change within your own company, great leaders keep on trying. They are never fearful of failure; they are always looking for ways to improve or do things in a new way.

Someone once said that you learn as much from failure as you do from success. In fact, Thomas Edison famously said, "I have not failed. I've just found 10,000 ways that won't work."

**About Andy Brenits**
Andy Brenits builds the playgrounds that creatives get to play in. An inspired design and creative business leader, Andy is accomplished at building and leading teams that deliver exceptional business results and creative ideas. He's passionate about the creative process and how it can be used to drive strategic business goals, and has been delivering thought leadership, creative solutions and design thinking for nearly 20 years.

Andy Brenits is the Creative Director at Arizona Public Service and serves as InSource President of the Board of Directors. This article was previously published at in-source.org.

**Remember the group critique?**

Way back when we were in design school, the group critique created the uncomfortable shifty feeling of being poked at for your design thinking and implementation. A hundred years later you're still sitting in that same seat, just in a slightly different way.

Each day we listen to the feedback our clients give us on the projects we present to them—some relevant and savvy feedback that helps propel the project forward and some not-so-helpful feedback.

Don't be afraid to push back when the critique is weak. When I say weak, I mean: "I just don't like it, can't tell you why, but I just don't like it." This, as we all know, is not constructive criticism; it's simply a waste of everyone's time.

Leadership requires insight to see the problems that need to be solved. Progress comes from understanding our clients' needs and style. Communicate with your clients. It's ok to ask for more detailed feedback. It's more than ok to say, "Can you elaborate on what you do not like and explain your vision to me?" It is rare that once you ask the literal question, you will continue to get the blow-off answer of "I just don't like it."

Let's face it. Our clients are busy, and most likely your project is not key to their existence. So do your best to steer them in the right direction, so you get the feedback you need and deserve.

Robin Colangelo

The Best Opportunities
Are Often Hidden in
the Shittiest Requests

-Bob Calvano

If there's one thing I've learned working in-house it's that there are plenty of roadblocks. There seems to be an array of never-ending obstacles and, at times, folks lined up just waiting to say no. Sound familiar? Truth is, it's not much different anywhere else. I've talked to in-house leaders all over the country, even some folks across the pond, and we are all dealing with the same problems.

In general, one consistent gripe I hear is that in-house teams get the "shitty" projects while the agencies get the "sexy" ones. I've heard people say, "We don't have the opportunity to..." blah, blah, blah, fill in the rest (you know how it goes).

As leaders, it's our responsibility to create opportunity—even when it doesn't look like there is an opportunity. That's easier said than done, so I'm going to provide you with some insight on how I've gone about creating opportunities—from the shittiest of requests.

We all know what these requests sound like. "Can you put a logo in the lobby?" Or how about this one: "We need to update last year's brochure. There's no need for a brief. Here's the new copy so just swap out the old images with these new images. Oh, and we need it done by next week." Really, you want fries with that, too? It's funny how folks always come to the design team with solutions, isn't it?

I can almost hear what's going on in your head. You're thinking things like "They don't value design," or "They don't value me," or "We don't do that."

When these phrases go off in your head, let that be a signal that you are face to face with a potentially golden opportunity.

I received a request to put a logo in a lobby once. It was one of those mundane orders that in-house teams often get and fulfill. My first thought was "Sure, I could do that, but you don't really need me to do it. I'm sure a local sign company would happily field that request. And besides, we're working on other stuff." I thought those things, but I didn't say them. What I did say was "Yes, I can put a logo in the lobby." But it didn't stop there. A golden opportunity awaited.

As leaders we need to be able to see beyond ourselves, beyond the implications for the self, and take a wider view. We need to think about what good can come from our creative talents. How can we be at service to others through design? How can we demonstrate the value of design and move business forward?

We also must be exceptional listeners. But you can't just be a good listener; that's not enough. The differentiator, the key to opportunity, is to listen with a very open mind, without judgment, and look to solve problems way beyond what is being asked. We also must be able to ask great questions—the right questions that get us to the core of the problem.

So after I said yes to this logo request, I went into question and listen mode. After my barrage of questions to stakeholders, I synthesized everything I heard and realized an opportunity presented itself. The lobby where a logo was needed was in a brand new office space. Guess what was in the space? Nothing. Well, nothing on the walls anyway. There was some furniture throughout the space.

What presented itself was the opportunity to do environmental graphics throughout the entire space. And then two big problems immediately presented themselves: 1) No one asked for that, and 2) My team didn't provide the service. Facilities planned to blow the dust off of old pictures that they had in storage and hang them (you know, pictures of lakes and mountains). I had a vision, though, and the passion in my heart assured me that I would provide a solution that would far exceed anything that was expected.

As a designer, I know one of my primary intentions for those I serve is to evoke their emotions. In this logo request, I saw the opportunity to emotionally connect people to the mission of the company. I wanted to connect people to their purpose for being in the space and to feel great about being there. I wanted people to feel proud to be a part of the company, its accomplishments and its contributions to society, and to reflect on the past while also keeping an eye on the future of the industry. There were no pictures in storage that could accomplish this type of storytelling.

I needed to put a pitch together, build some relationships and build trust among the stakeholders, and I needed to secure a healthy budget, if I was going to pull this off properly. Oh, and I also needed to recruit a few designers who could help me execute this vision. I also knew I had to take baby steps in order to get stakeholders to see the potential, possibility and benefits of doing a project of this scale within the office space. So I took it one step at a time.

During the process, people were lining up to tell me it was a waste of time, that I shouldn't focus on this type of work and that no one would really care about it in the long run. It was not part of my goals for the year, so it was an unnecessary task to take on. It certainly wasn't going to be factored into my bonus. And no one could see the work going beyond the one location. Thank God I didn't listen to any of this or make it mean anything. And thank God I had already learned a fat lesson about chasing money over my passion for providing great design solutions.

To make a long story short, we nailed it. But it doesn't end there. The result was the birth of an environmental design practice within the in-house studio. To this day, award-winning environmental graphics and sculptures are currently being installed all over the world. The service has caught the eyes of the senior-most leadership in the company and is one of the most valued services the in-house team has to offer. This has ultimately helped to change the perception of the team and has created even more opportunities. More importantly, it showed business people the bottom-line power of design.

And to think that no one asked for this blows me away—they didn't even know they needed it. What they thought they needed, and what they asked for, was a logo. But it's not what you hear that's important. It's what you are listening for as a leader of a creative team, who knows how powerful design can be, that matters.

As leaders we have the great honor and responsibility to lead. That includes not indulging your fears to the point where you concede to just filling requests. And many times it requires taking risks and failing. That can be uncomfortable and scary for many people. It's OK to be afraid, but it's not OK to let fear stop you from providing expectation-exceeding design solutions to business problems. A student recently told me that it occurred to him that I was not afraid to take risks or to fail. The truth is, I'm terrified every time. But the confidence I have, my passion for design and my trust that the opportunities for design solutions will reveal themselves to me enable me to transcend that fear more and more quickly with every shitty request I receive.

How do you get the confidence to do this? How do you transcend your fear of stepping outside your comfort zone? Well, that's a different chapter.

**About Bob Calvano**
Bob Calvano is the Vice President of Design at A+E Networks. He leads visual and UX design for A+E's portfolio of properties including A&E, Lifetime, HISTORY, HISTORY 2, LMN and FYI. Bob's focus is on the digital media side of the business, which includes executions on desktop, tablet, smartphone and emerging platforms such as Apple TV, Roku, Xbox, Amazon Fire TV and whatever comes next. Bob also currently holds a position on AIGA's National Board of Directors and plays a crucial role in determining the mission of AIGA.

**A customer service attitude**

If you have clients, then you need exceptional customer service chops.

All clients—internal and external—need a certain amount of care and handling to promote a healthy and successful relationship.

The best way to come across as flexible and position your team for success is to avoid saying the word "no." Instead, consider offering alternative options, otherwise known as compromises.

The word "no" seems to make people see red. After they hear that dirty little word, they hear just about nothing said after that.

Altering your approach by presenting options—such as "Well, I can offer this alternative angle, which fits your objective and stays on brand."—brings the discussion back to the strategy of the project and avoids the words that can halt progress and lead to frustration.

Try it out and see for yourself.

Robin Colangelo

# Building a Great Team

-Nathalie Heywood

Building a team is one of the biggest challenges for a manager. As managers, our first responsibility is to make sure work gets done. Getting the work done requires getting the best people and then getting the best out of them. To create the "great team" we need to be clear about our goals and expectations and understand ourselves and our leadership style. Then we can create a work environment that is in line with our goals, and make sure we have the right employees doing the right job.

The first step to building a great team is to identify your goals as it relates to the company. Your goals are a combination of the team's purpose, responsibilities, structure, culture and corporate values. Once you know what needs to be accomplished, you've got to figure out how to get it done based on your leadership style. For example, if you are a charismatic whirlwind that people just like, chances are you need very organized people on your team. If you are an organized and detail-oriented individual, you probably need a few big-idea people on your team.

The next step is assessing the strengths of your team. It's easy to identify the team members with standout strengths and a daily passion for their work. These employees are always improving their approach to their job and continually looking for new ideas, and because of their commitment, they end up pushing you to do better—such employees are your "A-Game" players. Other employees who you know are good, but you haven't figured out what to do with, are your "B-Game" players. So you need to decide if the rest of your team members can become A- or B-Game players.

For those who have yet to reveal themselves as A-Game or B-Game players, the simplest way to figure out if they belong on the team is to use the standard "three-strike method." Step 1: Discuss areas of strength and improvement, set expectations and a time frame. Thirty days is usually enough. Step 2: Meet to review the results. If they have changed behaviors, then you have a great team player. If not, give them one more chance and another 30 days to reevaluate expectations. At the end of 60 days, you both will know whether it's a partnership or time to say goodbye.

Now let's focus on the B-Game players. They are skilled, which means the main task is to match the goals and the structure with their skills. It's important to review expectations with them. You will find most of the time they just misunderstood what was required to be successful and needed clear feedback in order to adapt to the team dynamic.

For the A-Game players, it's important not to take them for granted so remember to validate their contributions and recognize they make the team unique.

Once you have assembled a great team it becomes a matter of keeping them. There are simple things you can do every day, such as acknowledging performances that go above and beyond. Pass on feedback from clients when things go well. When things aren't working, address it informally—don't escalate if you don't have to. Give thanks publically.

And for yourself, unless otherwise needed, set aside two hours a month to review your team. Jot down anything noteworthy for review once a month. The point is to have an accurate record, to keep it simple and be effective.

**Lesson learned**

I've been lucky to work with amazing people. Some of them I had to lay off or fire as a result of our business changing or because they had changed. Yet we still remain friends because we communicated regularly when things worked and didn't work. When there is clear communication, there are no surprises and limited upset.

**About Nathalie Heywood**

Nathalie Heywood is Vice President at Update Inc. She started the division Update Graphics, and oversees business development and strategy. She has created and executed thought leadership, reputation management and social media programs. Nathalie has helped professionals transition into new career paths, graduates embark on their careers and executives position themselves for emerging growth.

**Prioritizing**

It's no easy feat prioritizing these days. Email, voicemail, text messages, snail mail, questions from your staff, deadlines, new projects coming in, managing your clients expectations/questions/complaints. AAHHHHH!!!

Oh, did I say email? Receiving more than 100 emails per day is the norm and enough to make anyone insane.

So what's the answer? How do you prioritize all of these lines of communication that crash into each other all day, every day?

Keep a list—jot down all your to-dos, all the time. Check it several times per day. Be realistic about the list. The list could very well be 50+ items long. Do not overwhelm yourself by thinking if you can't get it all done in two days you're a failure. Choose the top three priorities each day and make them happen.

Sometimes you have to ask people to wait. You're the leader so you know which projects you can put on hold while you deal with crucial deadlines that must happen on that given day. So do it. There's nothing wrong with telling someone you can review their project with them tomorrow, so you can focus on today's priorities.

I believe successful prioritizers simply have the ability to explain to others that their tasks come after someone else's, in a sophisticated, articulate way that doesn't leave people feeling like second-rate citizens.

Robin Colangelo

# AKA Dad:
# Leadership Lessons
# From Parenthood

-Glenn Gontha

As a father, I have come to realize that most of the challenges I face as a Dad have direct parallels to leadership challenges at the office. Whether it's helping solve tough homework questions, coordinating elaborate school projects or playing the role of referee, DJ and car service provider—often simultaneously—it's a never-ending juggling act.

Taking the metaphor a step further, parenthood is an enterprise like any business, with success metrics (good grades and making honor roll), campaigns and rollouts (think book reports and shoebox dioramas) and the occasional curveballs ("Dad, I need poster board for a project due tomorrow"). With three very energetic sons, and over a decade of experience under my belt, I can rattle off a litany of valuable work/life lessons, but I'll focus on a few examples that I hope will bring perspective to challenges in team management and personnel development.

### Let them paint

I was in the middle of a home improvement project, painting a bedroom, and thought it would be a great idea to enlist the boys' help. I kept it simple, assigning them to paint closet doors. After I provided some quick pointers, they were off! It was clear very early on that this wasn't going to go as planned. Although they were doing their best, I couldn't expect them to execute as I would have. After four coats, a frenzy of paint drips and considerable cleanup, they did get the job done!

It took me a long time to learn the value of delegating. Early in my career I struggled with the concept, often thinking "I can get this done faster if I do this myself" or "My team will think I'm lazy if I assign this to them." New managers may feel the need to prove themselves and take on projects and tasks on their own. There may be some truth to these statements, but the negative impact to your team becomes more evident as your team grows and your responsibilities as a leader grow with it.

As a team leader, my responsibility is to empower my team to function at the highest levels possible. We are NOT order takers; we are consultants who add value every time we have an opportunity to sit at the table. Delegation reinforces the concept of "owning" the work. Like a complex machine, if one cog doesn't work, the entire system fails. Similarly, individuals need to own their "cog" for the success of the project. Giving team members ownership has long-term advantages:

+ Signals they have an important stake in the success of a project
+ Builds project and client management skills
+ Provides face-to-face client exposure
+ Encourages inter- and intra-team interactions and relationship building
+ Develops their management and communication style
+ Raises each individual's (and by extension, the team's) profile

Provide a framework for success—setting expectations, periodic check-ins and milestones—so your team member has a concrete understanding of how success will be measured for the project or task.

### "Fiddling" to your goal

My oldest son plays violin. Believe me, this wasn't one of those grandiose ideas my wife and I had about starting him early and becoming a virtuoso. He wanted a violin for Christmas when he was 6 years old. But the deal was this wasn't a toy; he would take lessons. Five years later, I am amazed at how well he can play. Granted, he hates practicing, but I remind him that he has a genuine gift.

It's been rewarding to witness how individuals on my team develop in their careers. They not only get better at what they do over time, but also their interests and skill sets evolve. And their growth isn't always predictable. For instance, someone who is a junior designer can find his or her calling on the account side because this person has a knack for liaising with clients and is super detail-oriented. Or when a project required animation but there was no budget for it, someone stepped up and learned it. It's imperative that my team work in an environment that encourages success and growth. I want to surround myself with the very best—experts who can answer questions that I can't, who I can rely on and learn from.

As the role of marketing and creative services evolve, our service offerings must also adapt. From print to digital, video to social, our roles demand being adept at marketing on multiple channels. Successful teams need people willing to expand their skill set to stay competitive, which often means wading into unchartered waters. Think outside of the box and find matchups with someone's interests, goals or past experiences. I've had firsthand experience of this during a video project. While I was discussing the project with a team member I was surprised to learn the individual had deep experience with film and video, having majored in the subject in college. I would have never thought of including this person in the project. So when building your project teams, look beyond the "usual suspects" or recast roles (within reason!) to bring a different perspective to the project.

### Roll with the punches

By far, the most valuable parenthood lesson for me is learning to adapt to any situation. As a parent, the only certainty is uncertainty, and the ability to think on our feet is something we do constantly. As your leadership responsibilities grow, you learn quickly that the work is the easy part. In a perfect world, all we'd need to worry about is coming up with great creative by a given deadline. And we all know that's rarely the case.

Whether it's my son or someone on my team seeking my guidance in a difficult situation, I always use the same approach: Give yourself time to think, assess all your options and act decisively. It sounds simple enough, but I know from personal experience how difficult keeping a cool head can be during crisis mode. Our value as team leaders is measured by our ability to deliver time and again, despite obstacles we encounter along the way.

The greatest gift of parenthood is that it's given me perspective. It's an enormous responsibility but one I am grateful to have. Although I've learned so much, I know there's much more to learn, which keeps the journey exciting. And, coincidentally, that's what keeps me going in my career, too!

**About Glenn Gontha**

Glenn Gontha is the Marketing Manager at Davis Polk & Wardwell LLP, an international law firm, where he leads a team of creative, digital marketing and content strategists who oversee the firm's branding, messaging and web presence. Glenn's background spans a variety of creative leadership roles, both in-house and studio/agency-side. He was a partner at re:creative, a full service design firm whose clients included prominent non-profit, cultural and educational institutions and technology, entertainment, financial and professional services organizations. Glenn received his B.S. in Design Studies from The State University of New York at Buffalo.

**Climate control**

What's the climate like on your team? Sometimes the answer depends on which day you ask me this question.

What do you do when your organization turns up the heat with a heavy workload and tons of conflicting deadlines? Stress can be a tricky thing to navigate through. But the older and wiser I become, the calmer I am in front of my staff, and I do believe that calm breeds more calm.

Remember that deodorant commercial, "Never let them see you sweat." Well, I think there's something to be said about that statement. The last thing your staff needs to see is a blown-out, aggravated leader. So here's a few suggestions to consider:

+ Keep it positive, even when you're doubting everything.
+ Jump in and get your hands dirty if your staff is drowning.
+ Host a lunch to allow everyone to take a break and step away for an hour.
+ Ask each person individually what their number-one pain point of the moment is and help them relieve it.
+ Keep stressors away. Meet with difficult clients, so your staff doesn't have to feel the negativity.
+ Remember to say please and thank you.
+ Complimenting your staff's work is huge and so often forgotten and overlooked. When people do good work, let them know. Letting them know in front of others is an added bonus.

Robin Colangelo

You've Got Superhuman, Telescopic Infrared, Bionic Gifts!

-Ed Roberts

I remember the moment my parents recognized my unique abilities. We were snowed in, no work or school for five long days. My big red balloon of eight-year-old excitement deflated to absolute boredom three days into our imprisonment. So I found a piece of paper, a pencil and an old family photo and began drawing.

Two hours later I gave the drawing to my parents for approval. As they quietly took in my interpretation of their likenesses, I noticed a strange mix of shock and awe flash across their faces. My mother, with drawing in one hand and phone in the other, called my grandmother excited. "Momma, Edward has a gift!" At the age of eight, hearing my mother's proclamation got me thinking, "What gift? I opened them all at Christmas and nothing's better than my Steve Austin Six Million Dollar Man action figure with telescopic infrared eye and bionic grip!"

Fast forward several decades, I'm sitting across from the CFO discussing the development of our latest annual report. I was confident in my preparation of each question, thoroughly anticipated his answers and formulated my rebuttals. Everything was going as planned until just after I asked my last question. I was totally caught off guard by his final comment, "You're on a different wavelength than I, in a good way. You're skilled at this, and it shows in the work." After the CFO made this comment I surveyed his face to see any signs of sarcasm. Oddly, what I saw was an expression similar to the one I'd seen on my parents' faces years earlier, except with an added mix of assured confidence and respect.

I left our meeting wondering if my unique abilities had taken a backseat. Had I forgotten those gifts that were encouraged by my parents, developed in design school, ultimately helping me land my first real job?

The short answer was yes. For the last 12 years my focus has been directed at building, motivating, inspiring and providing fuel to all those creative powerhouses operating under my guidance and supervision. I've also had to learn how to successfully navigate environments dominated by people who are less interested in creativity and focused more on the bottom line, while desperately trying to grasp that old brass ring. I've taken pride in being both creative and business minded. This duality has been a source of inspiration and strengthened me professionally.

The CFO reminded me that my natural gifts—although not omnipresent or at the forefront of my mind—are in fact on full display each and every day, influencing all the work produced by my department. In-house design managers have a tough and often thankless job. We are called on to make the impossible possible every single day. If you ever find yourself waist deep in corporate weeds or feeling as though you don't have enough fuel left to ignite the creative fire in your own belly, remember this: Like Steve Austin, you've got superhuman, telescopic infrared, bionic gifts!

**About Ed Roberts**

Ed Roberts is Creative Lead at ElectriCities of NC, Inc. and the director of marketing for InSource. He is also a writer, speaker and award-winning creative director who is an expert at constructing high-performing in-house teams comprised of creative superheroes. Ed explores topics on design, strategic thinking and corporate creative management.

This piece first appeared on HOW's In-house Designer Blog on February 23, 2012. Ed is also one of the programming partners planning the in-house management track of the 2015 HOW Design Live Conference. Follow him on Twitter @InHouseObs.

**Have a process**
"Creativity is subjective—the truth isn't." That's the clever new PSA from Advertising Standards Canada (ASC). Well, the truth is, creativity isn't that subjective, either. It's a process—as much science as it is art—and more often than not, ideas flow most freely when a project has parameters, guidelines and a process.

Too often, the work you produce is reduced to a matter of stakeholder taste. Clients dictate and creatives bemoan the restrictions placed on their work, constantly frustrated by the "if only" injustice of compromised visions: "I don't like brown." "Logo cannot be changed." "Can't we use all the white space on the page?"

Having a process and sticking to it avoids this unhelpful tug-of-war and the feelings of resentment it engenders—on both sides. Projects will vary in size, scope and creative latitude, but the process to arrive at deliverables should always be the same. Write a discovery summary document of the project goals and have everyone sign off. Now they have agreed to the critical inputs, timelines and outcomes.

Do your creative work, then tie it back to the summary document. Use everyone's signed-off words and directions as leverage to guide them to the right solution. But don't stop there. Follow up on the measures for success.

Now you've become a true marketing partner, not a tool in their toolbox. And there's nothing subjective about it.

Chris Davies

# A conversation

Working In-House With Academics: Past InSource Board member Kevin Kearns talks to Robin Colangelo about a day in the life of an in-house creative leader.

**RC   Describe what your team structure looks like.**

KK   Currently, we are structured to partner with internal departments to advise on strategy, planning and limited internal execution, as well as steer partners to outside vendors to fulfill deliverables. Projects we produce/execute internally are directly connected to our overall departmental high-priority initiatives, which are set a full year before.

**RC   How large is your team?**

KK   Our team is 11 strong, including seven writers, one designer, one web developer, one production manager and our Executive Director.

**RC   What type of work does your team produce for your organization?**

KK   Direct-to-donor materials that highlight and educate gift-giving opportunities. We develop far-reaching messages using social media, web and print publications.

**RC   Thinking back, what was your top challenge as a creative leader?**

KK   In an academic environment, it is important to gather a wide-ranging perspective and corral all opinions together to decide on a course of action. This is challenging because the scope of the project can take twists and turns, resulting in messages landing far from their original target. We are mindful that in some situations there are too many big fishes in the pond, and they don't always get along.

**RC   Where do you usually look for leadership inspiration?**

KK   I turn to peer groups and other internal leaders who have demonstrated a resolve in surviving the fatigue of an overstimulated over-opinionated base.

**RC**    **Do you have any leadership tricks of the trade to share?**

**KK**    Be open-minded and listen, then take the necessary time to make a decision and stick to it. I know it's simple, well-worn advice, but it works.

**RC**    **How do you continue to expand your leadership skills?**

**KK**    I read, listen, watch and absorb all that is happening around me. Then I apply what I learn to real projects and see how it goes. We forget that it's all trial and error in the end. If you don't try, you won't lead.

**RC**    **What do you like about being in-house?**

**KK**    The work-life balance!

**RC**    **What is one of your most memorable accomplishments?**

**KK**    Several of my television commercials for Bud Light were featured during the Super Bowl, one of which was named "one of the all-time greatest Super Bowl ads of the decade" by CBS.

**RC**    **Can you share advice you wish you had been given so you didn't have to learn the hard way?**

**KK**    You are not always right, all of the time. Listen as much as you can, then do the work.

**About Kevin Kearns**

Kevin Kearns is the in-house Art Director for Duke University in Durham, North Carolina. He leads creative development and execution of the Duke University brand for the 2012-2017 Duke Forward capital fund campaign. Previously, Kevin worked at DDB Chicago for 13+ years, where he was awarded a Lion at the prestigious International Cannes Advertising Festival. Kearns was vice president for InSource from 2010-2012, in addition to heading up the design and branding function for the non-profit.

Kevin is currently an adjunct professor at the University of North Carolina at Chapel Hill, teaching art direction and integrated marketing campaign development. He earned his B.F.A. from Miami University in Ohio and his master's degree in Advertising Design from Syracuse University.

# Managing In-House Design: A Better Working Process in Five Steps

-Brandie Knox

Great design—and successful designers—thrive on information and process. The creative process may seem free-form and spontaneous, and to some degree it certainly does need to embrace moments of pure creative thought but, in fact, it is only with information and a clear method that good design emerges.

When I first joined an in-house team in 2004, I noticed that the firm lacked an internal workflow process for the design team. There was a feeling that the design team could and should handle projects "on the fly." Projects came in without briefs or timelines. As a result, the team had no clear process for getting clear direction and working efficiently. Furthermore, every project was labeled "urgent" since the firm had never developed an understanding of how long the design and production process for any given project might take. In addition, they did not plan far enough in advance to ensure that projects could receive an adequate amount of attention and resources.

With information that is accurate, thorough and thoughtful, designers can know the Who, What, Why, Where, When and How of each design project. Who are we designing for? Who has the information we need? Who is approving the project? What content do we have? Where will the design live or be distributed? When are my critical deadlines? When will it launch? Why are we doing this now? How do we hope this project will alter the conversation about our business?

Process provides parameters, clear metrics and a way to check in with the goals and needs of each project.

The following simple steps will set your internal client's expectations, manage team workload and ensure a successful product.

## 1. Create project forms or a creative brief.

### Project forms
For small projects—event and seminar collateral, pitch materials, posters—use a short, basic project form outlining specific criteria for your project:
+ Audience
+ Medium (digital, mobile, print)
+ Size
+ Sign-off personnel and requirements
+ Content requirements (who will provide, proof and approve content?)
+ Project dates (internal sign-off dates, launch dates)
+ Production, distribution or publication method

### Creative brief
For larger, more complex projects, work with your client to determine goals and objectives, target audience and other key elements. This process need not be as extensive as a brief you might develop if you were within a design firm working with an external client since you have some understanding of the brand but, particularly with one-off projects, it ensures that you and your internal client are operating with the same ideas, goals and expectations of the approach and next steps.

A high-level, simple outline will help answer many upfront questions—often, your internal client may not have thoroughly thought through some of these questions. The criteria outlined in the form will ensure everyone is on the same page when a project gets handed off to another designer on the team. Get your project started on a positive note.

## 2. Establish a timetable.
Be proactive, not reactive. Work with your client to determine the timeline, including design and production, whether print or digital. This ensures everyone on the project team is clear on the required deliverables (yes, that includes your internal client) and is kept up to

speed when there is project creep. It also helps the client to understand going forward how much time needs to be allocated to any given project or a given phase of a project. Many clients need help factoring in the time required to work with external teams—writers, illustrators and photographers as well as printers, programmers and mailhouses.

With larger projects, a timetable helps you manage your entire workload, which also means that you can align your work process against foreseeable milestones in each project. With a clear project timetable, you can set expectations about when projects can start and how to distribute work among the team.

### 3. Present options.

It is incumbent on the design team to provide the internal client with options in the earliest stages of the design process. Depending on the project, this may mean developing multiple concepts or just a number of layout options. Presenting options ensures that you remain flexible in your own creative process, and gives the client the ability to see how the problem can be addressed in different ways. It also means you are less likely to have to "go back to the drawing board" as the client sees that you are actively considering different ideas. In addition, it occasionally establishes that one design direction is clearly preferable and can often get everyone excited and on the same page about a design.

Presenting two to three options is ideal (never more). But this is critical: These design directions should be presented to your internal client in the form of an in-person meeting. You should walk your client through your design choices and explain each option. Don't take the client into the weeds of your design process and every color choice, but give them an opportunity to understand why each design direction addresses the needs outlined in the creative brief. Give them the "why" and "how" of each direction. Then leave room for a lot of discussion. If your client is in another office, do this by phone or Webex, but do not simply send it by email and ask for feedback. Your dialogue with them is important.

## 4. Develop templates.

It seems obvious, but when I first went in-house there were no consistent templates for routinely produced materials such as event collateral, brochures and newsletters. Even now, I find many in-house firms I collaborate with lack templates or style guides. Developing a series of templates streamlines production time, ensures brand consistency and helps deter the client's inclination to art direct a single project or produce a one-off.

## 5. Establish a sign-off methodology.

Particularly for print production, I soon realized that "final sign-off" was a bit of a willy-nilly process. Who signed off before running a large print job? Who was responsible for approving final content? A simple sign-off form encourages a level of detailed review in the process. It can be fairly simple. Start with:

+ I have thoroughly proofed and reviewed the content
+ I approve the design concept
+ I approve the layout
+ I approve this final proof; production may proceed

Attaching this to your final proof, and requiring the responsible internal party to review and sign it typically prompts the internal client to review with a keen eye.

Expect that it will take some time—months or even years—for a new process to become firmly entrenched within the firm.

You may want to prioritize the rollout of each element or, alternatively, establish the entire process at once and present it to key stakeholders within your organization to ensure their buy-in, commitment and support of your team. In addition, establish regular check-ins with your internal client and design team to ensure that the process is working. If not, shift gears. Figure out what isn't working and why. Listen to your client if they are having difficulty with any element in the process.

The goal is not to add meaningless bureaucracy but to create a methodology that benefits all. A clear design process is the best means for ensuring that the firm maintains the integrity of its brand with its audience.

With a clear working process in place, you and your clients will find that design is a more enjoyable and successful part of running the business.

**About Brandie Knox**

Brandie Knox is Principal & Creative Director of Knox Design Strategy based in New York City. Knox Design Strategy specializes in corporate communications, brand identity, digital strategy and graphic design for professional services, financial and law firms. Before starting her own studio, Brandie managed an in-house brand and design team at an international law firm. The Knox Design Strategy team continues to collaborate and consult with in-house teams.

**Hold out for the right fit**

As leaders, we must follow our gut instincts because when we don't, it certainly comes back to bite us.

Years ago I was on the fence about transitioning an employee from another team into Creative Services. Sadly, I thought a warm body was better than nothing, so took the chance against my own better judgment.

What a dumb decision that was.

Not only was my initial instinct that the individual wasn't the right fit correct, but also the individual's shenanigans created a poisonous environment for the rest of the staff.

It took months of documenting and trying to correct bad behavior before HR was comfortable with me letting the person go.

So in the end, I created more work and aggravation for myself instead of holding out for the right fit.

Lesson learned.

Robin Colangelo

# New Brand Launch– What Is Your Internal Strategy?

-Cynthia Saccoman

You've spent months making changes to the logo, getting the colors just right, making sure your fonts are bold and modern, writing and rewriting your brand promise and what the brand means to your customers. You have incorporated all of the items into your new TV spots, radio spots and packaging, but did you think about your internal clients?

What often gets overlooked is how your employees, co-workers and internal clients are engaged, and the important role they can play in the branding/rebranding process. What does the new brand mean to them, and can they articulate it?

When launching or relaunching your brand, a solid internal launch strategy is just as important as your external launch strategy and the key to a strong, consistent brand experience. When properly informed and engaged, you can essentially have a brand army at your disposal. Your employees can be your biggest asset in expressing and conveying your brand promise.

Depending on the size of your organization and your reach, you have a multitude of options to execute your strategy. Here are some tactics to consider:

**Communication to your executive-level leaders**
Show them the value. Think about what your brand means to them, how a cohesive brand experience can help them and what it means for their branches of the organization. Consult with key stakeholders about what you can do to help them articulate the new brand to their staff and clients. Perhaps they need a more concise version of the brand guidelines with high-level talking points. Create the proper tools to keep them informed.

**Communication on a broader level throughout the organization:**
What are the communication channels that you have at your disposal to regularly get your new brand message out? Think about your employee newsletters. Introduce a regular brand highlight column to keep the brand top of mind and highlight the various ways the brand comes to life through the employees. Can you arm your department heads with more granular talking points relating the brand promise to their departments? In other words, how will this specifically impact one's department? Does it mean better customer service internally, or is it a motivator for more efficient workflows? Make it relatable—the more people understand the brand and what it means to them, the more they will be its champion.

**Taking the brand experience to your employees:** Let's face it, when working in a large organization, sometimes the volume of communication can be overwhelming. Your attempt at brand messaging can get lost in the inbox. Consider how you can take the brand to your employees in a fun, exciting way. Instead of your usual meeting with a PowerPoint deck showcasing the 75 new print ad versions, try organizing a brand launch party. Make it fun, brainstorm ideas—think out of the box. What would make sense for your organization? If your employees' first experience with the new brand is well, NEW, you will catch their attention and they will remember it. Another tactic to consider is organizing multiple brand launch events throughout the corporation to reach as many employees as you can. Go out with brand ambassadors who have immersed themselves into the new brand, who understand its meaning and how to articulate it. Have conversations with your employees, engage them, ask questions and educate.

**Keep your brand top of mind:** Make sure your brand strategy contains a communication plan that will continue throughout the year. It's not a "launch it and forget it" type of project. Reach out to your employees by keeping up with your newsletter articles or creating and refreshing an internal brand experience website. Invite your employees to participate in your brand activities. People love swag! Have brand contests and give away tchotchkes. Think of your employees as an additional channel for brand expression in the marketplace. Keep them well informed about the brand so they know it, love it, live it and breathe it.

When your employees understand and embrace the brand, the job of expressing the brand gets that much easier and becomes very apparent to your external clients. So when your new external brand is in its infancy, don't forget to also plan your internal brand strategy.

### About Cynthia Saccoman

Cynthia Saccoman has been a past board member for InSource and is currently an active member of the InSource community. She is an accomplished Art Director with over 20 years' experience in the in-house environment. She also loves painting and illustration and has two children's books currently in process.

# 2-minute tip

**How to ask for money**

If your college grad came to you and asked, "Can I have $250 dollars?" you would say no before she could even finish her sentence.

Now, what if the same kid went to her Dad and said: "I would like to join an organization of my peers so I can learn X for $250." Don't you think she's going to get a yes answer? Yep.

Put everything into context when you ask for budget, tools and staff. Prove the need, the savings or the added benefit to the organization and professional development for you and your staff.

If you can put some logic and strategy behind the spend, you'll be surprised at how often you hear YES.

Robin Colangelo

# Working With External Vendors

-Chris Davies

I'm a double agent in the marketing and design world. For 13 years, I was the in-house creative director for a major financial services group. Then I jumped over the wall and opened my own agency. For the past 15 years, I've been the lead dog at my company, Dog and Pony Studios. But I'm only a stone's throw from my old in-house neighborhood.

Almost all of our work involves partnering with creative directors of in-house marketing groups. Having worked both sides, I have a clear picture of the professional practices that lead to lasting, productive relationships, as well as the mistakes and oversights that derail projects at the get-go.

As a vendor, I see how the work we produce amplifies our clients' brands—and the reputation of the creatives in charge of them. But back when I worked in-house, I had a love/hate relationship with agencies. If we had to farm a project out, I would worry that I'd look like I wasn't pulling my weight, or failing to deliver through my in-house team. I worried my team would be seen as incapable, or even worse, unneeded. Moreover, it seemed that vendors had a way of working on the more exciting projects, whereas we were tasked to produce a never-ending pile of everyday things. (To be fair, we had a lot of exciting projects, too, but the high pile of the everyday items always made them seem few and far between.) On top of it all, I was frequently cast in the role of the vendor's sherpa, leading some outside creative director over mountains of paperwork and processes while dodging predatory stakeholders. If not for me, they would have been lost (and likely have starved to death), but I felt I could never take credit for the work produced.

Still, I recognized that vendors were an invaluable lifeline to delivering complex projects (or ones that needed to appear overnight). They augmented our team with specific skills that weren't part of our day-to-day work and brought fresh perspectives and approaches to our brand. The best vendors were partners who added a lot of value, while making my job easier.

Here are my thoughts on facilitating great partnerships with outside agencies, so you and the brand you represent can get the most out of working with external vendors.

### Why outsourcing is empowerment, not defeat

The first thing to understand is what outsourcing can do for you. Outsourcing can empower you to deliver more, faster (and better). It can also be the best use of your budget; no matter how modest, you have a budget and you need to show value for it. Vendors are an extension of your team, not a replacement. Remember: All businesses hire contractors across all areas of practice—so why not yours?

At the most basic level, outsourcing can give you access to specialized skills, such as back-end coding, mobile web development, SEO or social media management, app development, custom illustration, video production and more. Many of these skills aren't needed on a day-to-day basis, so, of course, it's not part of the in-house capability. But when you get a call from the CFO who thought they'd Google the firm—and you came up on page five—you need an SEO specialist, pronto. Enter vendor.

Beyond these specialized skills, vendors provide a fresh, experienced perspective on your brand. Perhaps you need to redevelop the brand voice by coordinating your key differentiators across your tagline, elevator speeches and other copy points. Expressing the values of a brand is difficult when many of those values are part of what you do every day as an employee. You're just too close to see it clearly, and you need new eyes. Vendors can see the trees rather than the forest (or the forest if all you see are trees).

### Establish who is going to manage the project

There's no hard and fast rule about who should be the project manager. It's entirely dependent on the nature of the project. That said, there can be only one project manager: you, or the vendor. Ask yourself: Do I have processes and experience with this kind of assignment to manage it properly, or is it better left to the vendor?

No matter who manages the project, however, a clear project plan needs to be in place. It doesn't have to be complex, just clear. Define who is doing what activity, who is providing the content, who is editing it and other roles. With added players comes added potential for miscommunication. Setting up the project in a simple but powerful tool such as Basecamp can help to keep track of all communications and provide a digital paper trail, especially should aspects of the project start to go sideways.

### Educate each other on workflow

Your vendor needs to understand the usual workflow for projects. If your colleagues (and more importantly, bosses) are used to a certain cadence, now is not the time to change their expectations. Tell your vendor where the usual touch points are for sign-off (discovery/research, outlines, wireframes, scripts, full drafts). Of particular importance is the workflow expectations for the gorilla stakeholders, such as senior executive "final review" (which is typically their first review), or review by legal and compliance. The workflow and process of handling input and direction from these stakeholders is critical to a project's success, since their input can often come in at the 11th hour and has the potential to derail months of hard work.

With all this information in hand, your vendor can then integrate their best practices to your workflow to keep things moving smoothly on the inside, without sacrificing the methods that have made them successful and skilled in the great big marketing world outside.

### Establish where you stop, and they begin

Even with roles and responsibilities defined, you still need to get granular in areas that may have grey zones. The more sharp lines you can draw, the fewer friction points that will materialize during the project. Think about where the hand-off point will be for things such as creative latitude for brand standards, fact checking and editing copy. Who is responsible for securing domain names or hosting? Is the vendor sourcing images? Do you have a budget for licensing stock art or do you have a library they should use?

### Share the office politics (that matter)

There's a lot to be said for the off-the-record lunch. Of course you need to keep some things close to the chest, but it's in everyone's best interest for you to flag personalities or informal channels that will influence the outcome of the project. The goal is efficiency. You don't want your vendor wasting time navigating office politics or mediating longstanding internal disputes. Let your vendor know who you report to and don't use them to even scores.

### Discuss budget up front

Vendors want to make a good margin on the work. You want to protect your budget. Making these two goals meet can be tricky. How do you approach it? Start by calculating how long your project would take you and your team (if the task is within your capabilities). The calculation will give you a ballpark estimate on costs for comparison. Ask your vendor for a realistic price, given the scope, timeline and other factors (such as politics) that may influence edit cycles and delivery. Don't squeeze your vendor down in price to save pennies, but don't allow a vendor to take advantage of your budget because the timelines are tight, or because your brand is a Fortune 500 company. Be frank and open. It's best to get the financials sorted out quickly, up front and in detail.

### The vendor's job is to make you look good

Your company has entrusted you to spend its money, deliver a product on time and ensure your brand is at its very best. No pressure, right? Well, no pressure for you. It's the vendor who is responsible for delivering on time, on budget and on brand. Make sure your vendor understands that anything less will damage or end their relationship with your firm, no matter how much you may like them. And it'll damage your own reputation, too, if they deliver over budget, late or an underwhelming product. Their job is to ensure this project isn't a lose-lose for themselves and for you.

### Your job is to make them look good

If you follow the advice given here, you will have done your job to give your vendor everything they need to succeed and look like stars. When the project closes, don't forget to give credit where credit is due. Recognize your vendor as the engine behind the brilliant product, and give yourself credit as the driver. The recognition will set the bar of expectation high for any future work with your vendor—and it gives them credibility among your colleagues, which will make it easier to get sign-off when you wish to use them again in the future.

**PS:** Don't forget to establish all the miscellaneous rules of engagement Outside of these major sweeps, there are other items you'll need to consider, such as:

+ Non-disclosure agreements: Do you need to protect your firm's information?
+ Portfolio and case studies: Can your vendor showcase the product, or are they to be a ghost designer?
+ If you can openly discuss your partnership, how can you mutually use social media to amplify the reach of the work—and your business—in the process?
+ Copyright: Is it clear who owns the product?

+ Reuse of code: If the project is digital, can your vendor use it in the future, or is this code proprietary to your firm?
+ Source file turnover: Do you want the files, and if so, what formats and software versions do you need?
+ Other random practical things that can derail a project at a critical time, such as IT blocking the use of Dropbox or other issues that can stop delivery when the clock is ticking.

## Vendors are partners

I opened this saying I was a double agent in the marketing and design world, but that's a bit of a misnomer because it implies sides, when really, there are none. Everyone is on the same side, and the goal is to deliver excellence.

Creativity isn't produced in a vacuum. So take advantage of the oxygen an outside agency can breathe into your brand. Make use of their expertise. Recognize the value they can add to your job. Give them the tools they need to put their best work forward. Empower them to take ownership of the project and fully engage their creative and critical faculties.

Above all, treat them as partners. It's a simple practice that costs nothing but has big returns. Because—as we all know—in business, relationships are everything.

### About Chris Davies

Chris Davies is the founder and creative director of Dog and Pony Studios, a marketing agency providing solutions to all major Canadian banks, and has successfully built brands for all manner of businesses, including international companies, tech industry start-ups, and professional associations. Prior to founding Dog and Pony Studios, Chris worked 13 years at the Toronto Stock Exchange, from the trading floor to creative director. With over 25 years of experience on both sides of the in-house and vendor relationship and thousands of projects under his belt, Chris is an expert at seeing the big picture—and attending to all the details that put every last pixel of the big picture in place.

## Budgeting

I am often surprised to hear that many in-house creative leaders are not running their own budgets for their departments. And because they are not the budget owner, they have very little say into what and how much goes into the budgeting process.

We all know running an in-house creative team is similar to running your own design studio. You have staff costs, hardware and software costs, paper, toner and professional development costs—just to name a few common line items.

Even for small teams under five people, this is a lot to track and manage properly, so why would you want a noncreative leader managing the creative budget for you? Well, you don't, so speak up.

If the creative budget in your organization cannot be broken out separately from the marketing budget, then at least get involved. Let your boss know that you would like to review a line-itemed budget for the following year so you can assist in controlling it throughout the year.

For those of you who have trouble getting approval for conferences, membership fees and professional development initiatives, here's your chance to plan for it, get it in the budget up front and let your boss know what it's all about way in advance.

Robin Colangelo

# Three Things Successful In-House Creative Leaders Do Differently

-Joe Staples

In my 18 years of marketing leadership experience, I have had the opportunity to work with and manage several exceptional, insanely creative leaders of in-house creative teams. In my current role as CMO at Workfront, I have the unique opportunity to regularly meet with and observe creative leaders at top companies around the world.

What my interactions with and observations of creative teams has taught me is there are everyday creative directors, and then there are successful creative leaders—and successful creative leaders do, in my opinion, three things differently:

**1. They don't fear process.**
Creative types, by nature, tend to resist (and sometimes even abhor) the very idea of "process," feeling that structure inhibits their ability to be creative. Because of this mindset, there are creative teams all around the globe that live in constant chaos—with requests flying in from all different directions, constant interruptions, disconnected work management tools, insane workloads, little-to-no visibility about who is doing what or when projects will be delivered, disjointed communications with the team and the internal clients, multiple fire drills per day, never-ending rework, exhausting approval and revision rounds—you get the idea.

All of this chaos, however, keeps creative teams stuck doing administrative work (such as attending daily or weekly status meetings, navigating email back-and-forths) and takes away from time they could be spending on delivering creative work. Instead, they work nights and weekends to hit their deadlines, and ultimately, job satisfaction and team morale dwindle. All this, because the team lacks structure. I have noticed that successful creative leaders don't fear process. They believe in balance. They understand that a standard set of processes (such as creative briefs

and project or workflow templates) can not only save time, but also keep work in balance—so creatives spend less time planning and coordinating, and more time keeping their creative
juices flowing.

## 2. They don't fear numbers.

Studies have shown that in-house creative teams consistently list gaining respect from internal clients and proving their value to peers and executives as their biggest challenges. But creative types aren't usually keen to spend time on spreadsheets or data crunching, so how can creative teams realistically prove their value and gain the respect they truly deserve?

The successful creative leaders I've observed may not like numbers, but they certainly understand their impact. And not only that, they understand that numbers can help them prove the value they contribute to the department and to the company. They help their team members see the value in accurately tracking their time—as these numbers not only can increase productivity, but also make it easier to estimate project deadlines and build trust with stakeholders. They also track deliverables: How many projects did we complete last quarter? How many of them were delivered on time? What can we do better next quarter? This intel helps creative leaders prove to executives and
clients that work is getting done, and it's getting done well.

## 3. They keep an agency mindset.

A more recent trend I've noticed is that successful in-house creative leaders are stepping up their game. They've singled out their external-agency competition, and they're committed to outperform and out-create them. They do this by thinking and operating more like an agency. Many top-notch in-house creative teams are now doing things such as:

+ Renaming their team from "Creative Services" to "The Studio" or "The Agency".
+ Restructuring their team to function more like an agency—complete with account managers who interface with internal clients.
+ Offering a standard set of services to internal clients or choosing a specialty.
+ Adopting chargeback billing structures to create a more agency-like experience as well as to keep clients accountable.

By adopting an agency mindset, in-house creative leaders are pushing their teams to stay competitive. They're winning pitches and opportunities to work on more interesting work. They're winning awards over their agency counterparts. Successful in-house creative leaders are creating a world where in-house creative teams are just as cool, attract just as much talent and are just as forward-thinking as agencies.

Every creative director wants to do something to set himself or herself apart from the rest. Many try to do this by coming up with extremely creative ideas and focusing on winning awards. But successful in-house creative leaders, I believe, take some of their creative genius and apply it to how they manage and structure their teams. They don't accept the status quo. They don't buy into the notion that creative life will always be chaos. And when they challenge these beliefs and do things differently, the results speak for themselves.

**About Joe Staples**
As Chief Marketing Officer for Workfront, Joe Staples leads a best-in-class marketing organization focused on building the Workfront brand and driving awareness, thought leadership and demand generation.

**Building blocks**

Having built out many teams over the years, what I know for sure is this: You cannot spend enough time training and communicating at the beginning of the process. People are generally in a state of confusion until they "get it."

My best practice is to spend as much time as I can explaining, reviewing, setting the tone and explaining again.

How do you fit all of this into your day job? You just do. There's always a 10- to 15-minute window you can find in your day to squeeze more into. And in the end it's so worth it.

I find myself maxing out my day with lunches and dinners just to make it all work. Hey, if it doesn't work, it's my butt, so I better get savvy with my time.

The part, for me, that seems to never get easier is finding great people. I'm talking about the kind of people who are such pros and an amazing pleasure to work with. I'm talking about grown-ups who know how to get it done and not get stuck in the mud. They're out there, and I'm proud to say I have many on my team after years of searching, but it never gets easier finding new ones.

Robin Colangelo

# Avoiding "Death by Committee"

-Angela Buchanico

Committee—the dreaded word that elicits visions of endless meetings, memos and members. The death knell for any project. If you work in an in-house environment, this is a pretty common scenario. I had that perception from the agency side. But that was nothing compared to what I would face in-house at an institution of higher learning.

By definition, a committee is a group of people who are chosen to do a particular job or to make decisions about something (source: http://www.merriam-webster.com/dictionary/committee). It is perceived as acceptable and necessary for launching an initiative by a specific group of knowledgeable employees for the good of the institution or company. But the reality can be much different, especially if you are charged with creating one and you're not prepared. A poorly formed, ill-functioning committee can launch your project straight into purgatory. But, if approached in a strategic way, it can position you for success.

Here are eight steps to building a great committee, establishing momentum and bringing your project to life:

### Step 1: Be aware.
Know which projects are important to your institution and to you and your team. The more you understand how your particular environment functions, from the top down, the more likely you'll be ready when the time is right for your project. Join forces with those who have a stake, particularly at the executive level, and encourage them to advocate for you by showing them how much it means to their success. When my time came, I was able to step into the void to move the project forward, and be associated as an indispensible part of the project.

### Step 2: Do your homework—first.

Because I was quite close to the project that I brought forward, I was aware of the challenges and felt compelled to act, as any success would impact my team the most. By researching other approaches, in other environments, and then forming an outline of best practices specifically relevant to my project, I was already prepared. I had possible solutions, a framework to guide the committee selection and some creative ideas to reach our desired outcome.

### Step 3: A lean, mean team.

Include those who benefit most by a successful outcome but who can also handle the commitment. By developing an outline that showed where the pain points were, and what results mattered most, I could see quite clearly which departments and individuals to include. Smaller is better. It will be necessary to loop in ad hoc members with specific skill sets on a limited basis. Resist the temptation that everyone remotely connected to the project participate as a full committee member. This bloating will doom any progress, possibly any success, and bog it down with irrelevant, tangential tasks.

### Step 4: The WORK.

Define a reasonable and actionable charge. And stick to it! Always refer to it throughout the process to stay on track. Then determine the scope, the schedule and the funding, specifically where the money can/should/could come from. Then define success measures. If you followed step 1, you already have a sense of what success looks like. Step 4 is a LOT of WORK. And it varies by project. But it will prepare you for effective engagement. Delegate tasks, which shouldn't be challenging if you follow step 2. Ask committee members to hold each other accountable for their work. Finally, establish reasonable but firm deadlines. Everyone is busy. Try to anticipate any roadblocks by allowing some flexibility in the assignments and the timeframe. Cushion as much as possible but within reason.

### Step 5: Engagement and buy-in.

Take the temperature of your environment. Assess where heads and hearts lie. You will need internal champions and cheerleaders, as well as external thought leaders and experts, as advocates. Engage via surveys, open forums and even one-on-one sessions with those who want to participate, especially those who have the most to say (both positively or negatively). Hear what is being said. I have found that sometimes an objective external consultant can advance the goodwill of a project more than anything else.

### Step 6: Analyze/Audit/Assess.

Encourage constant feedback within the committee and among constituencies. Collect and analyze as much relevant data as you can find. Audit any existing content. Assess the internal and external competitive environments. Be selective and simplify as much as possible. Relevance is key. This will help keep the committee engaged, and discourage sidebars, tangent projects and deviation from the charge.

### Step 7: Share often.

Find ways to report back on every level, in a manner relevant to every audience. Establish a blog. Utilize social media. Communicate the status of the project consistently. Engage the champions to provide feedback along the way. Not every detail needs to be shared—only those milestones that have meaning. I've found that this creates the energy and excitement that can propel the project forward at critical stages.

### Step 8: Propose.

The committee should be well prepared to create a succinct, actionable proposal. Create a sense of urgency at this time. Reach out to garner support before presenting to the executive team. Be prepared to answer all questions and defend every detail.

Outline the specific next steps needed, including the desired approvals and funding recommendations. Be specific about what is being requested, whether it's an RFP, a brief or a blueprint. Your project is now ready to move to the next level.

### About Angela Buchanico

Angela Buchanico is assistant director of marketing at University of the Sciences (USciences) in Philadelphia, PA, and a self-proclaimed process fanatic. A seasoned and award-winning creative, she has built diverse teams and brought organization to both agency and in-house environments. Angela is a novice writer and blogger, interested in topics on design, organization and creativity. She is also a budding entrepreneur, partnering in an independent dance music label, 418 Music.

**Redefining brilliance**

All projects are not created equal. Some projects have the right brief, budget and timeline to make it possible to promise—and deliver—excellence. Others, not so much. There's a saying in our business that you may have heard: "Cheap. Fast. Brilliant. Pick two."

Two of the three parameters can bend. Some timelines have flexibility. Sometimes more budget can be found. But brilliance is the one thing that you never want to sacrifice.

So what do you do when you're facing a project that demands brilliance, but there isn't enough time, budget or both? Your best course of action is to remind your client that they need to pick between fast and cheap if they want brilliance. Ask questions: Is the deadline tied to a real-world hard stop or is it more about someone wanting to cross a project off their list ASAP? Is there a budget to allow a trusted agency or vendor to assist?

And who knows? Maybe brilliance can be redefined. After a chat about time and budget you may come to the conclusion that you can pull from your existing inventory of brilliant material and resolve the issue without forgoing your professional standards.

At the end of the day, your job is really about solving problems and adding value, which means that sometimes you showcase your brilliance as much in how you handle projects and clients as in how well you do the work itself.

Chris Davies

# A little back story

In 2002, realizing that there were almost no opportunities for dialogue, training and support for inhouse design directors and managers, a group of in-house leaders formed InSource to establish an association committed to addressing those issues.

InSource moved quickly to provide a venue for initiating dialogue, and in 2003, InSource held its very first roundtable event that included a powerful presentation by Peter Phillips of the Design Management Institute, a respected expert on in-house management. The discussion was followed by the attendees speaking about the challenges their departments were facing and brainstorming solutions to those challenges.

The excitement among the participants at having this opportunity to share ideas and strategies for improving their departments was clear, and InSource began to develop plans that would further its mission.

You can read more about our history in the October 2013 article published in GDUSA: 10 Years Later: Where We've Been & Where We're Going.

**in-source.org**

62037427R00046

Made in the USA
Columbia, SC
28 June 2019